13

Essential

Spells

A collection of spells for every Witch.

Leandra Witchwood

ISBN: 9781976926129

Independently published

I dedicate this book to you.

You are the seeker of wisdom.

You are the architect of your path.

I hope my words of wisdom and years of experience serve you well.

Bright Blessings,

Leandra

Magick

Magick is in your heart

It is woven into the fabric of your life

Magick is the essence of your soul

It is the flavor of life taken one bite at a time

Magick is the color of flowers blowing in the wind

It is the gentleness of the sunset

Magick is the fury of the sea

It is the sturdiness of bone

Magick is yours to weld

It is your blessing and burden to bare

Magick is yours to cherish

Table of Contents

Introduction

This book is a collection of 13 spells every Witch should have in his or her library. Each spell is simple to perform. Each spell uses easy to find ingredients to support the simplicity of each working.

You can use this book as a baseline for creating spells that are tailored to your unique style of practice and magickal needs.

I offer you a variety of techniques throughout this book, from Candle Magick to the use of herbs and crystals. The variety within this book will give you a sense of the diversity you can incorporate into your practice.

How do Spells work?

Spells work because you have your head in the right place and you are focused on success. When you seek to perform a spell make sure you have your attitude in check and that your focus is keen.

What is the difference between a Ritual and a Spell?

While the words Ritual and Spell are often used interchangeably, there are subtle differences between the two.

Spell work is usually a type of ritual where a specific outcome is created or expected. Within a spell, you will use your will, emotions, psychic & mental focus, and often specific ingredients to manifest change or influence energies to work in your favor.

A ritual can also include a spell but traditionally observances to mark a rite of passage, a point in time, or a celebration. A ritual is also an act or sequence of actions you perform on a regular basis.

In this book, I do not offer any specific instructions related to how you should prepare yourself and your sacred space. This part of magick and ritual is up to you. Creating sacred space is a personal experience. If you choose to take a ritual bath before going into sacred space - feel free to do so. If you feel the need to call and cast circle to help create sacred space - do so. The beauty of witchcraft is that you can tailor it to your specific needs and preferences.

A Spell for Grounding

There are many times in our lives and our magickal practices when we feel like our energy is all over the place. This is why it is important to become conscious of your energy. This spell will not only help you gain mental focus it will also prevent others from manipulating or interacting with your energy, whether it be intentionally or inadvertently.

Ingredients

A large bowl

Several stones, river rocks are a good option

Sand

Instructions

When you are ready to place your hands in the bowl and say:

Chaotic energy ground and stand,

within the stones, within the sand,

Calm and sooth each sacred hand.

Bring me center once again.

Repeat as necessary, until you feel your energy become relaxed and drawn back to you.

Honoring the Ancestors

"Our futures are built on the back of those who came before us."

Each of us has a rich support system that is rarely seen. Taking time to honor our ancestors helps strengthen our bond with those who came before us.

Ingredients

A white candle

A small offering plate or bowl

An Apple

Instructions

Find a place outside where you can sit comfortably for a few minutes and set up a simple altar. You can choose to make this altar permanent if you like, and I am sure your ancestors will not object.

Place the white candle on the altar and light it. Next, place the offering bowl or plate on your altar.

As you position the apple on the altar plate say,

Ancestors, I welcome you to this space.

May you continue to guide me on my path.

I leave you a gift. May it refresh and make you joyous.

Before leaving the Apple and the dish, say a little prayer to your ancestors and thank them for their support. Express to them what they mean to you and how you value their support.

Leave your offering on the altar for at least 24 hours.

Divination Tea

Use this tea before you perform Divination. It is particularly useful to those who often read cards, auras/energy bodies, dowse, scry, and more.

Use the whole dried versions of each ingredient to create your tea. Measure by weight not volume.

Ingredients

½oz Dried Orange Peel

¼oz Star Anise

¼oz Clove

¼oz Bee Balm

½ inch piece Celery (you may use less if you like)

Instructions

Mix the ingredients and store in an air-tight glass container for up to 6 months. Remember to label it for clear identification.

Brew the tea as needed with 2 cups of boiling water and a 1-1½ ounce measure of the dry mixture for about 5 minutes.

Use a tea strainer to remove the solids and enjoy before you perform any form of divination or readings. Sweeten with raw honey to taste if you wish.

House and Home Blessing

Make your house a home with this gentle blessing to welcome your energy. You may also take this opportunity to invite helpful spirits who will help you fill your home with positive energy.

Ingredients

1, White Candle

A candle holder you can carry

Clean Water

A shallow bowl

Lavender essential oil

Instructions

Mix about five drops of the Lavender essential oil with the water in your bowl.

Light your candle.

Begin in any room of your home by holding the candle up to each corner of the room. After you illuminate, the corners take your hand and dip it in the oil and water mixture.

Sprinkle the oil and water mixture in each corner, moving to the center of the room, and then out the doorway.

Repeat for each room of your home.

Happiness Spell

We all want to be happy. Some days we just need a little boost to get there. You can burn the incense on a charcoal puck whenever you need a pleasant boost in your day.

Ingredients

   1oz Lavender Flowers, dried

   ½oz Catnip leaves, dried

   ½oz Marjoram leaves, dried

Instructions

Mix each ingredient and store in an air-tight glass container. Remember to label it for clear identification.

When ready to use, light a piece of lump charcoal or a charcoal puck and sprinkle the mixture over the coal.

Personal Cleansing Bath

Once a month and before rituals it is a good idea to conduct an energetic personal cleansing. This cleansing will help you clear out the baggage or muck Magick users, and intuitive folks tend to collect.

Ingredients

1, Bay leaf

A 2" piece of raw coconut with the outer husk intact

½oz dried Lemon Peel

A reusable fabric tea bag or bath sachet/pouch

Instructions

Place all the ingredients into your pouch or bag. Run a warm bath and place this bag with the ingredients inside in the water as the tub fills.

Soak in the tub allowing all the energetic or psychic clutter you have weighing you down to flow away from you and into the water.

Remain in the tub until the water begins to feel cool. Drain the tub, remove the pouch and discard the contents.

Dream Tea

We dream every night. Studies say we have up to 6 dreams each night. Remembering the important dreams is key when you are searching for synchronicity and messages.

Ingredients

½oz Jasmine flowers, dried

1oz Green Tea

¼oz Rose petals, dried

¼oz Thyme leaves, dried

Instructions

Mix all the ingredients and store in an air-tight glass container for up to 6 months. Remember to label it for clear identification.

Brew this tea as needed with 2 cups of boiling water and a 1-1½ ounce of the tea mixture in a tea strainer for about 5-6 minutes. Sweeten with raw honey if desired.

Drink before you go to bed and keep a pen and paper or a dream journal near you to record your dreams.

Re-Charge Your Creativity

Creativity is essential to a Witch's way of life. We rely on our ability to see past the obvious and mold objects and situations to our liking. When your creativity feels like it is waning, give it a boost with this simple spell.

Ingredients

A pen

A piece of paper

A yellow candle

A fireproof bowl or vessel

Instructions

Go to a place in your home where you tend to feel creative. This place can be your craft studio, writing desk, a spare room, or even the kitchen table.

Take out your pen and paper, and light your yellow candle.

Write on the paper an affirmation related to your creativity. It should be positive and progressive like: "My creativity is abundant and flows to me effortlessly."

Next take this paper to the doorway of your creative space, along with the candle and light the paper. Drop it into your fireproof vessel and allow it to burn completely.

The Fresh Start Spell

We all come to points in our lives and spiritual practices where we feel a deep need for a fresh start. Maybe you have fallen into a rut and need to make things exciting and new once more, or you have been contemplating a project or a goal you need to complete. This spell uses Knot Magick and a simple chant to get the ball rolling.

Ingredients
Black or White String or Twine

Instructions
To start tie 4 knots down the length of your string or twine. Place the string or twine in your dominant hand and think of the project you would like to start or the area in your life where you need a fresh start.

Next, lay out the string or twine and take the first knot in your fingers.

Untie the 1st knot and say: *My guiding spirit will show me how*

Untie the 2nd knot and say: *to mix things up here and now.*

Untie the 3rd knot and say: *Take my hand and help me make it so,*

Untie the 4th knot and say: *My future is bright with a radiant glow.*

Altar Dedication & Blessing

Most Witches have an altar in just about every room of their home. Each altar has a unique focus. When creating a new altar, it is an excellent idea to dedicate it to the purpose it will serve and bless it toward your intentions.

Ingredients

Moon Water

A bowl

A white candle

An object or symbol representing the purpose of this altar

Instructions

Bring the ingredients to your altar, including the symbol or object you will use to signify the purpose of your altar. For example, if your altar is dedicated to the Goddess then add a Goddess statue. If our altar is dedicated to healing, then you might want to decorate it with some healing herbs or crystals.

Light your candle and place your item or object on the altar. Begin sprinkling the item and the altar with the moon water as you repeat.

I dedicate this altar to thee, (insert to whom or what you dedicate the altar).

Blessed Be!

Charging A Magickal Item

Often, we favor a piece of jewelry, stone, or object. Sometimes it is because this item was a gift from a loved one or it just has a special resonance. When you find an item like this, you can choose to charge it with additional energy for a variety of reasons, such as protection or healing.

Ingredients

An item you value

A piece of white cloth

Instructions

Perform this spell during the full moon.

Think of the type of energy you plan to charge your item with and hold your item in your hands as you think of this power. Place the item near a window on top of the white cloth.

This location should be where the moonlight can shine on your object for at least 1 hour.

Remove the object before sunrise the next day. You can use it immediately or store it in black cloth for later use.

Creating Magickal Barriers

It is important to learn to set barriers not only in the mundane sense but also in the energetic and Magickal sense.

Instructions

You can create your Magickal, psychic or energetic barrier anytime you feel the need.

Take a few deep breaths, and envision a white bubble forming from the top of your head and extending down to below your feet.

When you feel protected, you can then go about your business as needed.

Perform this as often as necessary.

Recovering a Lost Item

I hate it when I lose something, especially when it is an important something. When you lose an item, and you have searched everywhere for it, use this spell to help you locate your lost item.

Ingredients

A piece of crystal quartz

A piece of white cotton cloth (large enough to hold your crystal)

White twine or string

Instructions

Hold your crystal and repeat:

Lift the veil from my sight,

find what I seek on this night.

Between the sky and the ground,

what was lost can now be found.

Place the quartz in the center of your piece of white cloth and draw up the corners. Tie your cloth closed with the string or twine. Carry it with you always, even when you sleep.

Pay attention to your dreams because the location of your missing object might be revealed to you while you sleep. You may even feel the crystal vibrate or give off some extra energy when you are near your missing item.

Thank You!

I am blessed to know you have made this book part of your library.

I invite you to join our community online, on Facebook, and on Instagram!

Please remember to leave a review on Amazon about this helpful book!

Find me online:

www.TheMagickKitchen.com

www.LeandraWitchwood.com

About the Author

Leandra Witchwood -

Master Herbalist,

Reiki Master, Witch,

Earth-Centered Minister,

Teacher, and Author.

Knowing the difficulties many aspiring Witches face, Leandra has dedicated much of her life to teaching the essentials of Witchcraft to those who seek the esoteric knowledge of this path.

For over 20 years Leandra has looked to nature, the elements, and spirit to guide her on her magickal and spiritual path. Her education and experience are influenced by traditional, ceremonial, and modern Witchcraft; where the worship of nature is vital. Leandra teaches a multi-faceted perspective that provides each of her students with the means create his or her unique style of practice.

Leandra is the founder and writer of *THE MAGICK KITCHEN,* a food & lifestyle blog, and the co-founder of F.I.R.E. an earth-centered spiritual organization.

Learn more about Leandra Witchwood online:
www.LeandraWitchwood.com

Want MORE?

Get your copy on Amazon today!

Spell Work Notes

Takes notes on the spells you perform will help you gain wisdom and perspective in your craft. As you look back you will not only find areas for improvement, you will also see where you were most successful.

Use the following note pages to write about each spell you perform.

Spell Work Notes:

Spell Work Notes:

Spell Work Notes:

Spell Work Notes:

Spell Work Notes:

Spell Work Notes:

Made in the USA
Columbia, SC
15 June 2020